HOW CAN I STOP
WORRYING?

✖CULTIVATING BIBLICAL GODLINESS

Series Editors

Joel R. Beeke and Ryan M. McGraw

Dr. D. Martyn Lloyd-Jones once said that what the church needs to do most of all is "to begin herself to live the Christian life. If she did that, men and women would be crowding into our buildings. They would say, 'What is the secret of this?'" As Christians, one of our greatest needs is for the Spirit of God to cultivate biblical godliness in us in order to put the beauty of Christ on display through us, all to the glory of the triune God. With this goal in mind, this series of booklets treats matters vital to Christian experience at a basic level. Each booklet addresses a specific question in order to inform the mind, warm the affections, and transform the whole person by the Spirit's grace, so that the church may adorn the doctrine of God our Savior in all things.

HOW CAN I STOP
WORRYING?

GERALD M. BILKES

REFORMATION HERITAGE BOOKS
GRAND RAPIDS, MICHIGAN

How Can I Stop Worrying?
© 2018 by Gerald M. Bilkes

Reformation Heritage Books
2965 Leonard St. NE
Grand Rapids, MI 49525
616-977-0889
orders@heritagebooks.org
www.heritagebooks.org

Printed in the United States of America
18 19 20 21 22 23/10 9 8 7 6 5 4 3 2 1

ISBN 978-1-60178-642-5
ISBN 978-1-60178-643-2 (e-pub)

For additional Reformed literature, request a free book list from Reformation Heritage Books at the above regular or e-mail address.

HOW CAN I STOP
WORRYING?
—✘—

Be careful for nothing, but in every thing by prayer and supplication with thanksgiving let your requests be made known unto God. And the peace of God, which passeth all understanding, shall keep your hearts and minds through Christ Jesus.
—Philippians 4:6–7

We all worry. Rich people and poor people worry. Those who are educated as well as those who are uneducated worry. Young people worry, as do older people. Single people worry; married people worry. Those in high-tech societies worry, and those in less industrialized countries worry. People at every level of society worry. People who believe the Bible worry. People who don't believe the Bible worry. Worry is something that affects all of humanity.

People worry about all sorts of things. They worry about their money and jobs. They worry about their social prestige and their reputation. They worry about their safety or health. They worry about the world and the church. People worry about their children and their parents. They worry about getting married and about staying married. People worry especially about the future. Perhaps because our past is already behind us and we can't control the present, we have the illusion that we can somehow control the future at least.

Some people do worry more than others. Trauma in our past or present or simply the inability to handle a lot of tension or insecurity can play a role in anxiety. Yet most people know what it's like when their mind spins around the cares of the day and of tomorrow.[1] Although we realize that many of our worries in the past haven't come to pass, some of us continue to live with daily anxiety, constantly fearing the present, fearing the future—things that are or things that never will be. The Bible is so realistic and also practical and strengthening. It lays out for us a gracious path for bringing our worries to God and trading them for a deep peace through Jesus Christ that can fortify and guard us, regardless of our circumstances, enabling us to bring glory to God.

WORRY IS FRUITLESS

What has anyone accomplished simply by worrying? When has it lightened life's load? When has

---

1. For some people, anxiety can be so severe and immobilizing that they need concentrated care and counseling. Please discuss your anxiety with a qualified counselor if this applies to you.

it changed the outcome of a situation? When has it erased the wrinkles on our brow and added a single day to our life? As hard as it is for us to admit, worrying is ineffective at changing any of our circumstances for the better. Instead, worry breeds more worry, less confidence, frustration, and panic. It is actually worse than unhelpful—it is harmful! As Charles Spurgeon said, "Anxiety does not empty tomorrow of its sorrows, but only empties today of its strength." In other words, worrying about tomorrow ruins today. It depletes its victims' physical, emotional, and spiritual strength and potentially spreads harm to others as well. Think about how worry has failed to help you and those around you. Has worrying brought you closer to Christ? Has worrying made you more of a cheerful witness to those around you? Has worrying inspired your unbelieving family members or neighbors to seek God?

Are we agreed, then, that Paul's teaching in Philippians 4:6–7 should be absolutely vital to our thinking? Are you receptive to this truth and how it should change the way you live? If so, come with me to the place where we learn this truth.

PEACE BEYOND HUMAN PEACE

Why do we need to be told not to worry? The Scriptures make clear that God wants Christians to know the peace of God in their hearts. This peace goes beyond human peace. It is more than just a personality trait or disposition of character. It is not calm that we bring to ourselves at times when we need it most, nor is it something only to be known during happy and carefree times. As we will see, Paul, the author of these verses, passed through "many dangers, toils, and snares"; in fact, he wrote these verses in Philippians 4 from prison. Is it possible, then, that we might really experience a peace that is shatterproof?

On the surface, the idea that peace ruling our hearts during even very difficult times could appear wishful thinking, a naïve idealism that simply dreams away worries or boxes them up and forgets about them for a while. Perhaps you think that living with deep peace is something only a few people, the most mature and seasoned Christians perhaps, might hope to experience. It is important for us not to push the truth of Scripture away from us or think that we are outside the reach of its truth, either because of our personality or circumstances. There may indeed be additional challenges for us with certain personality types, a set of circumstances in our lives, or patterns of thinking we have developed. There will also be ups and downs in how we experience this peace that God promises. Paul was a man of "like passions as we are." He knew what it was to despair even of life (2 Cor. 1:8).

What is more, this is not just Paul's teaching. It is God's word, not just in one place but given to us repeatedly. See the following verses from both the Old and the New Testament that address the subject of worry.

Thou wilt keep him in perfect peace, whose mind is stayed on thee: because he trusteth in thee. (Isa. 26:3)

The LORD is my light and my salvation; whom shall I fear? the LORD is the strength of my life; of whom shall I be afraid? (Ps. 27:1)

Take therefore no thought for the morrow: for the morrow shall take thought for the things of itself. (Matt. 6:34)

Be careful for nothing. (Phil. 4:6)

Let not your heart be troubled. (John 14:1)

These things I have spoken unto you, that in me ye might have peace. (John 16:33)

Casting all your care upon him; for he careth for you. (1 Peter 5:7)

For God hath not given us the spirit of fear; but of power, and of love, and of a sound mind. (2 Tim. 1:7)

Many of these verses are promises that spur believers to greater faith in God or commands that imply that God cares profoundly and constantly for His people. We ought to keep these truths before us, clutching them tenaciously.

But, you might ask, if God means for me to live like this, why isn't life easier? Why do so many confusing circumstances come my way? Why are situations so hard to figure out? Why does so much go wrong? If our lives were easier, we think, we would worry less, have more peace, and be able to trust God more. Or would we?

WARRIOR WORDS

Clearly, we cannot simply brush aside Paul's words as those of a youthful, untested optimist. Instead, Philippians 4:6–7 are the words of an old, rugged warrior who knew more pain and suffering than most people. Perhaps few if any of us could claim to have passed through more trials and tribulations in life than he did. He tells us a little of what he went through in 2 Corinthians 11:23–27:

> In stripes [I am] above measure, in prisons more frequent, in deaths oft. Of the Jews five times received I forty stripes save one. Thrice was I beaten with rods, once was I stoned, thrice I suffered shipwreck, a night and a day I have been in the deep; in journeyings often, in perils of waters, in perils of robbers, in perils by mine own countrymen, in perils by the heathen, in perils in the city, in perils in the wilderness, in perils in the sea, in perils among false brethren, in weariness and painfulness, in watchings often, in hunger and thirst, in fastings often, in cold and nakedness.

Take another moment to read through this list. What horrible circumstances Paul went through! Think of how many times his life was in danger. Think of the suffering he had to endure. As already noted, Paul is *in prison* as he writes these words: "Be careful for nothing, but in everything by prayer." Humanly speaking, Paul is alone and uncertain of his future, facing trial and perhaps death. If this man can write a text like this, then he surely must have known the peace that "passeth all understanding" (Phil. 4:7). Paul understood how this peace of God can come into our hearts, dimming and dispelling worries as we exercise faith in the promises of God through Christ.

WE SHOULD CARE

Paul's exhortation that the believer be anxious for nothing has been interpreted in various ways, and the text is sometimes misapplied. Let's look first at what this exhortation does *not* mean.

When Paul says, "Be careful for nothing," he is not teaching that we should just have a carefree attitude toward life. As we saw, it's easy to think that this lack of worry must be connected to easy and happy living. Many people try to maximize the easy and the happy parts of life, attempting to squeeze out their difficulties by doing so. "Let what will happen, happen," they say. "All will turn out right in the end." Or "*Carpe diem*"—that is, "Seize the day." Many people live by this ideology, and some even seem to be successful as a result of just having a generally positive though humanistic attitude to life. But the Bible nowhere sanctions a careless attitude to life. In fact, the following are things about which we should care deeply.

Our Souls and Their Salvation

The Lord Jesus says in Matthew 6:33, "Seek ye first the kingdom of God, and his righteousness; and all these things shall be added unto you." This familiar verse is part of the Sermon on the Mount (Matthew 5–7), in which, among other things, the Lord Jesus teaches the futility of anxiety by turning His disciples' focus on the character of God. He especially emphasizes God's loving, heavenly care for His people (e.g., Matt. 6:25–34). In other words, the Lord Jesus makes clear that instead of being occupied with self-centered care, we should be concerned to please God and seek His kingdom. That should be our first concern, and if by grace it is, then we will find that all our true needs will be provided for. We will lack nothing that is good and necessary for us (Ps. 23:1).

This does require faith in the character of God as well as in His promises. There will be testing times when our faith will be tried and stretched. Elijah's faith was tested when the brook where he had found sustenance during a famine ran dry (1 Kings 17:7). Yet even these times of testing are good for us if they refine our faith and make us look with more steadfastness and expectation to God as our heavenly Father. Why would we worry when the Father in heaven has wealth and riches in His house (Ps. 112:3)? If we are believers, servants of this King, then Matthew 6:33 is a great promise to which we can cling. We can come to the throne of grace and lay all our cares and needs before God, knowing that He has promised to provide for those who love Him.

Avoiding Sin and the Traps of Satan
The Christian life is a battle. Believers are called to fight against powerful enemies—sin, Satan, and the old man who lives within. It is frightening to realize how vulnerable believers still are to the attacks, devices, and schemes of Satan. He will tempt us to sin and to dishonor God's name. He will tempt us to leave the narrow way on which we are called to walk and to leave the battlefield and admit defeat. Therefore, believers must live in a constant state of watchfulness and vigilance. As Peter says, "Your adversary the devil, as a roaring lion, walketh about, seeking whom he may devour" (1 Peter 5:8). Therefore, believers must live in a constant state of watchfulness and vigilance. They are to exercise much care not to dishonor or disobey their Master or to bring shame to His cause. Isn't it ironic that Satan uses worry as one of his great traps for the believer? He distracts our thoughts from God to the thoughts of the world, and we so easily follow his lead, misdirecting our attention toward the cares of the day. We so easily move our focus from the things that really matter.

Our Various Fields of Responsibility,
Aiming at the Glory of God

God has given each of us responsibilities to fulfill in the various positions in which He has placed us. We need to discharge these duties with great diligence and with an eye to the glory of God. Slackness and carelessness should have no place in our work. Parents should take great care in raising their children in such a way that God is glorified. Employees should take great care to work in such a way that God is glorified. Officers in the church should take great care as they labor in the cause of Christ. Paul speaks in 2 Corinthians 11:28 about how he felt "the care of all the churches" resting on him. Paul knew that believers are called to be the body of God in the earth, His hands and His feet, caring for His cause. Paul felt responsible both for his own conduct and for that of the churches, so that the name of God would be glorified rather than dishonored and so God's cause and kingdom would be advanced.

So there are important areas in our lives that call for our great care and concern, and they are all related to the kingdom of God and His holiness. God deserves our care, love, and utmost devotion as we fulfill the responsibilities He has given us.

STEWARDSHIP

Paul's words "Be careful for nothing" also do not mean that we shouldn't take reasonable measures regarding our lives and the future. God has called us to be stewards of all that He has given us. The Bible consistently encourages wise, godly, intentional living and warns against laziness and thoughtlessness. Think about how we are encouraged to be like the ant. Like this little insect, we should work diligently to store up for the future (e.g., Prov. 6:6). The wise man instructs the farmer to sow his seed in the morning and not hold back in the evening (Eccl. 11:6), thus spending his investment and time wisely. Surely we have a responsibility to do our best in any given situation, both with our money and our time. Remember the story of the two builders in Matthew 7:24–27. Both men were building a house. The house built by the man who was careful and diligent stood firm through the storm, while the house built by the thoughtless and poor planner was easily destroyed. Taking proper care of the things of this world is necessary, and God calls us to do so properly. Paul wrote of his continual care for the churches (2 Cor. 11:28), using the same word to describe this godly zeal that Jesus used to forbid sinful anxiety.

So where lies the balance? How can we distinguish right care from wrong care? Matthew Henry has helped identify one difference as the *motive* behind the care. He wrote, "There is a care of *diligence* which is our duty, and consists in a wise forecast and due concern, but there is a care of *diffidence* and *distrust* which is our sin and folly, and which only perplexes and distracts the mind."[2] In other words, we can distinguish between proper and improper care largely by examining the *motives* behind them. If we worry about something because we are not trusting God, then we are doing wrong. If we worry in such a way that we become perplexed and distracted from our daily work, we are doing wrong. Henry explains that we ought to "avoid anxious care and distracting thought in the wants and difficulties of life. It is the duty and interest of Christians to live without [such] care. Be careful for nothing, so as by your care to distrust God, and unfit yourselves for his service."[3] So first, Paul is targeting a care that grows out of distrust or a lack of faith.

A second difference between right care and wrong care is *proportion*. John Sharp, a preacher in the late 1600s and early 1700s, wrote that what Paul is censuring in this passage is

> when we take more care to be rich, than we do to be good: when we study more to get a reputation amongst men, than to approve ourselves to God: when we are solicitous to get out of the present evil circumstances, in which we perhaps are, than to avoid eternal damnation.[4]

2. Matthew Henry, *Commentary on the Whole Bible, vol. VI-II: First Corinthians — Second Timothy* (Woodstock: Devoted Publishing), 231. Emphasis mine.

3. Henry, *First Corinthians — Second Timothy*, 231.

4. John Sharp, *Works*, vol. 4, *Sermons*, 5th ed. (London: T. and T. Longman, C. Hitch, and L. Hawes, et al., 1754), 8.

This becomes practical. Sharp warns against neglecting our daily devotions because we want to do better in our business and neglecting communion with God because we are more concerned to be popular with our friends.[5] Our first and great concern should be the glory of God. We should fear God and serve Him. If everything else is subordinate and subservient to that great aim, we will have the right focus, and that will help us put things in perspective.

On the other hand, wisely looking ahead to the future, proper planning, and careful execution of our responsibilities are behaviors to which God calls us. What is crucially important is that we are to do these things while looking to the Lord in all things, trusting in Him and in His wise and governing providence over all areas of life.

PRESCRIPTION

When doctors write out a prescription, they are advising us to take some dosage of medicine to help cure us. So too Paul, after giving us a prohibition, gives us a prescription. In other words, Paul isn't simply telling us *what not to do*; he tells us *what we should do*.

You might be able to imagine how difficult it is simply not to worry. Tell a child who is dreading the start of a new school year not to worry, and he won't be able to do it. Tell the anxious parents of a rebellious and wayward teenager not to worry, and they

---

5. Sharp, *Works*, vol. 4, *Sermons*, 12–13.

will find themselves powerless to take your advice. The human brain simply keeps bending toward the concerns of the mind and reaching out toward that which lies ahead. And we know how difficult it is to break a bad habit in life if we do not replace it with something better. But here is the brilliance of Paul's Spirit-inspired instruction. He tells us what we should do when worries invade our thoughts: "Be careful for nothing, but in every thing by *prayer* and *supplication* with *thanksgiving* let your requests be made known to God" (emphasis added). We must not just stop worrying. We must do so by replacing our anxiety with prayer, supplication, and thanksgiving to God that is grounded in faith in His character and promises. Let's look at these words in turn: *prayer*, *supplication*, and *thanksgiving*. These terms contain a rich theology of prayer. What does Paul mean by each of them?

Prayer

Prayer, at its heart, means making specific requests to God for the sake of Jesus. To pray means to look away from ourselves to God, on whom we rely and depend. It means that we believe that He exists and that He rewards those who diligently seek Him (Heb. 11:6). Paul directs us to prayer when we are anxious. He wants us to see how anxiety in our lives should be a motivation to pray. If the time I have spent in my life on disquieting worry had been spent in quieting prayer, I would have spent a lot of time praying! The thoughts you expend on furious worry need to be invested in fervent waiting on God. Have you ever seen your cares as invitations to prayer? The affliction in your life as a trigger for supplication?

Perhaps you are anxious and do pray—often and a lot. My experience tells me that many of God's children who worry a lot also pray a lot—more even than those who do not worry. This is proof, in a way, of the value and validity of Paul's instruction.

Maybe you are afraid that your prayers aren't good enough. Sometimes we can let our worry spill over and ruin everything. We worry that our prayers aren't true prayers. If you find yourself thinking like that, remember that true prayer need not be perfect prayer; there is sin and shortcoming in everything we do. God will not despise the prayers of His people, however, not even their sighs and groans. He accepts His people not on the basis of their prayers but on the basis of Jesus Christ, their ever-living High Priest, and His finished work. And because of Jesus, He will hear their prayers. True faith may be mixed with unbelief, so much so that we need to pray: "Lord, I believe; help thou my unbelief" (Mark 9:24). But let's pray in faith (James 1:6) and ask God to grow our faith (Luke 17:5). A good guide for believing prayer that God accepts can be found in question 117 of the Heidelberg Catechism:

First, that we from the heart pray to the one true God only, who hath manifested Himself in His Word, for all things He hath commanded us to ask of Him; secondly, that we rightly and thoroughly know our need and misery, that so we may deeply humble ourselves in the presence of His divine majesty; thirdly, that we be fully persuaded that He, notwithstanding that we are unworthy of it, will, for the sake of Christ our Lord, certainly hear our prayer, as He has promised us in His Word.

When by faith we are "fully persuaded" that He will hear our prayer, according to His faithful promise, then our faith triumphs in a measure over unbelief. We might not feel like victors; we might lose our nerve again and again. The confidence we have one moment might be shaken the next, yet God does not leave His struggling children to themselves. They can rest on the promise of His assistance.

The Canons of Dort have a marvelously encouraging section for those who struggle with doubt and the weakness of their faith in the fifth head, article 11:

The Scripture moreover testifies that believers in this life have to struggle with various carnal doubts and that under grievous temptations they are not always sensible of this full assurance of faith and certainty of persevering. But God, who is the Father of all consolation, does not suffer them to be tempted above that they are able, but will with the temptation also make a way to escape that they may be able to bear it (1 Cor. 10:13), and by the Holy Spirit again inspires them with the comfortable assurance of persevering.

This "comfortable assurance" is exactly what we long for when we are deeply affected by anxiety and worry, and God has so much of it to give.

Supplication

Next, Paul mentions supplication. By that he means further entreaties to God, more earnest and fervent petitions. The Bible speaks about a holy wrestling with God in prayer, like Jacob did when he asked for a blessing from the angel who fought with him (see Gen. 32:22–32; Hos. 12:4). When we don't receive an answer after our first request, we ought to continue praying, provided we are praying for things that are lawful according to God's Word. Paul prayed three times that the thorn in his flesh might be removed (2 Cor. 12:8–10). Jesus instructed us that we should do more than "ask, and it shall be given you" (Matt. 7:7). He went on to say, "Seek, and ye shall find; knock, and it shall be opened unto you." In other words, don't stop after asking once. Continue supplicating like a beggar who really needs to have what he or she is asking for. Or, to use another picture: like a child, don't stop asking your heavenly Father for the Holy Spirit, which He desires to give His people (Luke 11:13).

This kind of supplicating prayer is what Bartimaeus raised when the crowds tried to silence him as he called out for the Savior to show him mercy. We read that "he cried the more a great deal" (Mark 10:48). An even better illustration of supplication is what the Syro-Phoenician woman did when it seemed like the Savior gave her the cold shoulder (Matt. 15:21–28; Mark 7:24–30). She would not let the Savior go without hearing from Him the answer: "For this saying go thy way; the devil is gone out of thy daughter" (Mark 7:29).

God often delays answering our prayers because He is testing the sincerity of our desires, refining our faith, or readying us to receive another blessing from His providing hand. Whatever God's reason is for delaying—and often we never find out the reason—the proper response is to supplicate earnestly and submissively. Often when we supplicate, we find our prayers become more focused on grace to follow God more fully in our lives than for the specific thing we were asking for. Whether the Lord chooses to answer our supplications as we wish or differently from what we hope, the process of supplication is important and blessed for our souls.

Thanksgiving

Paul was in prison when he wrote Philippians, but his heart was very thankful (1:3; 4:10, 18). No wonder the letter to the Philippians is so joyful. In 1 Thessalonians 5:18 Paul challenges us to be thankful in everything. By reminding us to be thankful in every-thing, Paul is doing something strategic. The first place that thanksgiving has in our prayers is that it acknowledges God as the giver of everything. It honors God to thank Him, and He loves and deserves to be honored to the highest degree. Sometimes we can be so occupied with what we don't have that we forget all we do have and have received. Surely we can't forget that God will "give His grace and Holy Spirit to those only, who with sincere desires continually ask them of Him, and are thankful for them" (Heidelberg Catechism 116). Let us not be like the nine lepers who never returned to thank Jesus for healing them (Luke 17:11–19). Surely that is dishonoring to God.

Paul's instruction is strategic in a second sense, for it is encouraging and settling for us in prayer to remember all that God has done for us. There is always much to be thankful for, and when we remember even just a little of what God gives us, even in our darkest hours, these thoughts can give us hope for the unknown future (see Hab. 3:17–19). It also shows a Christlike spirit, which is pleasing to the Father. On the eve of His suffering, Christ remarkably thanked the Father (Luke 22:19). On his journey to Rome to testify before the emperor, after a shipwreck and many other dangers and difficulties, Paul "thanked God, and took courage" (Acts 28:15). Shouldn't we, then, live lives of thanksgiving to God, no matter what state or situation we are in?

Clearly, Paul's theology of prayer was rich and deep and provides normative instruction for us. If we follow it, we will find our faith deepened and our patience strengthened; and God will be honored on our account as we unburden ourselves.

PROTECTIVE PEACE

Paul does not just leave us with a command; he attaches a glorious promise to his command. He writes: "The peace of God, which passeth all understanding, shall keep your hearts and minds through Christ Jesus" (Phil. 4:7). It is a promise of peace, which is most fitting. For worry is the lack of peace; God's provision is peace.

In the Bible peace is an important concept. It's not simply the absence of war; it is the state in which things are right (Rom. 5:1), especially with God. At the instigation of the devil, we rebelled against God in our federal head, Adam. From that moment on, there was no peace with God. By nature we are at war with God, and God is at war with us. We are His sworn enemies. There can be peace, but only through Jesus Christ, who has come to reconcile sinners to God through His one sacrifice on the cross for sin. This peace is not anything the world can give, but Christ gives it by the gospel in our hearts (John 14:27). Through believing the record God gives of His Son in the gospel, we are reconciled to God. God says this: "I know the thoughts that I think toward you, saith the LORD, thoughts of peace, and not of evil, to give you an expected end" (Jer. 29:11). This is not just a nice, warm-feelings-based peace. It is a real peace that governs our lives through trust in God's provision and protection.

Paul doesn't just promise peace but notes that this peace will keep our hearts. Notice this important word *keep*. Literally, the word means "safe-guard" your minds and hearts. The idea is of a garrison that surrounds our hearts and protects it from attack. Without such a garrison, our hearts would be open to assault after assault. But steadiness and stability come through this peace of God applied to our hearts by the Holy Spirit.

If you have fears about the future, God invites you to lay them before Him, leave them there, and see how He provides. Are there fears for today? Pour out your heart to God, tell him all your concerns and anxiety, and you will find peace. Listen to how Paul puts it: "The peace of God...shall keep your hearts and minds through Christ Jesus."

You might be thinking, "This sounds simplistic. I wish it were that easy!" Or perhaps you say, "I have prayed, but the worries hang on. Nothing seems to change!" During worrisome times, we often feel that we're missing a sense of safety, security, and control. We may wonder, Who is going to protect me? Who is going to help me? Sometimes our situation is so dire that we despair. The fog is so thick that we see nothing of God's hand in our lives. Our worries stand between us and God and seem to close off any avenue of help. We cannot pray, we cannot read the Bible, and we cannot take in the comforting words of our brothers and sisters in Christ.

One reason prayer sometimes doesn't seem to help is because we don't leave our cares with God. Imagine that you give a friend a present and say, "I give this to you; it is yours to keep. But I still want to use it. I'll come whenever I need it and take it back from you for awhile." What kind of gift would that be, and what kind of relationship does this reflect? It is essentially an issue of trust, isn't it? If we take our cares back, we believe that either God isn't powerful enough to do the right thing or that He is not willing to do the right thing. At the very least, we fear that one or both of these things are true. Worry is indeed very closely connected with our view of God, isn't it?

Meanwhile, Paul gives us the right view of God that we should have as well: "The peace of God will safeguard you!" Notice that Paul· doesn't say that God *will* do everything we ask. He says that God will safeguard us. This is even better than what we often ask for because we often don't know whether what we ask for will really be for our ultimate good. But God promises to shield His people. This is exactly what the word *keep* means in this verse. Another way to translate it is "garrison you," "hem you in," "protect you." Think of Elisha and his servant, who were staying in Dothan when the Syrian enemy sent a great host to besiege the city (2 Kings 6:15–17). When the servant saw what was happening, he fretted and worried. It was as if he had eyes only for the Syrian army surrounding the city and saw no possible escape from their predicament. He cried out: "Alas my master, what shall we do?" It was a question of panic, and we can understand that, given the hopeless situation.

But Elisha responded differently to the situation. He said to his servant:

> Fear not: for they that be with us are more than they that be with them. *And Elisha prayed*, and said, LORD, I pray thee, open his eyes, that he may see. And the LORD opened the eyes of the young man; and he saw: and, behold, the mountain was full of horses and chariots of fire round about Elisha. (2 Kings 6:16–17, emphasis added).

Doesn't Elisha model for us what Paul is prescribing? This is what Elisha did: with prayer and supplication, he made his request known to God. This is what God did: the peace of God kept their hearts and minds. God gave a special gift to Elisha's servant as he opened his eyes; what he saw took away his worries. He saw the army of God that was stronger than any enemy and stronger than his own fears. Elisha and his servant experienced the garrison of God keeping them in perfect peace. Scripture tells us of others who were given the peace of God when it was most needed. Think of David, who lay down and slept, even in great difficulty (Ps. 3:5). Think of Paul and Silas, who were able to sing in prison

(Acts 16:25). We have every encouragement to look to God, who is the source of the peace that we need in the midst of all troubles and trials.

THE CALM AT THE FEET OF JESUS

If there were a school that would really help us push back on and overcome worry, don't you think many of us would want to enroll? And while it's not a physical building, there is one place where we can really come to know the peace we have been thinking about. It is sitting at the feet of the Lord Jesus, like Mary did in Luke 10.

The contrast between Mary and Martha that is sketched for us in this well-known passage (Luke 10:38–42) is stark but at the same time beautiful. While Martha was "cumbered about" (agitated with) all the things that needed to come together and all that needed to be done, she became irritated with her sister, Mary, who had a quietness and peace she didn't. Finally, Martha blurted out to Jesus: "Lord, dost thou not care?" (v. 40). Notice Martha's use of the word *care*. It was as if she wanted Jesus to worry like she was and to put Mary into the same frenzied mode she was in. But Jesus resisted the temptation to spread Martha's worry and anxiety and impose it on Mary. Instead, He diagnosed her illegitimate care: "Martha, Martha, thou art careful and troubled about many things" (v. 41). Her mind was restless because it had been distracted from the "one thing needful" and was scattered in other directions (v. 42).

Instead of just leaving Martha in the bondage of distractibility, worry, and stress, Jesus took the peace that Mary was enjoying and opened it up for Martha. He says, as it were, "Martha, here is the secret. Sit at my feet like Mary is doing. That is what will give focus to your life. That is what you really need. You need to deal with the many things out of the one thing, not let the many things push away the one thing." He invited her to the school of worry-free living at His feet.

To stop worrying involves more than just listening to Jesus as teacher. It also means depending on Him and trusting in Him as Savior. It is really learning to live out of the suffering and death of the Lord Jesus on our behalf. It is there that we find not only a *mental* peace, as Jesus teaches through His Holy Spirit, but, even more profoundly, a *spiritual* peace that addresses the deepest need of our souls in relationship to the God from whom we departed when we fell in Adam in the garden of Eden.

It is in the school of Calvary, the school of Jesus's suffering and death on behalf of sinners, where we learn over time, with falling and rising again, how it is that we can put off worry and experience God's peace. Consider the following God-appointed means.

Look to the Suffering Lord Jesus Christ

I know of no better place to look to learn the truth of this passage than the Lord Jesus Christ. He suffered like no one else has ever suffered. He had more reasons to be anxious than any of us. All hell was set against Him. The whole course of human history depended on him. All of His people's salvation rested on His shoulders. One misstep on His part and all would have been lost.

"Yes," you may be thinking, "but Jesus was divine too. He had power that I don't have." Indeed, He was, but He had a truly human nature, subject to weakness, fatigue, and all afflictions. He had not only a human body but also a human soul. On one occasion, in the garden of Gethsemane, he was "sore amazed, and…very heavy" (Mark 14:33). He was so sorrowful, so full of anxiety, that blood came out of His pores. The knocks on the door of His life were infinitely more ominous than what we experience because they carried the weight of the world with them. Yet see how Christ responded in the midst of His worries. He fell on His knees and prayed. He shared the troubles of His heart with His Father and submitted to His will. And what happened? "There appeared an angel unto him from heaven, strengthening him" (Luke 22:43). A peace that passed all understanding came from His Father above, and He was strengthened. Jesus's moment of intense anxiety exhorts us that "in everything with prayer, and supplication, with thanksgiving, let your request be made known unto God."

One of the blessed effects of Jesus's suffering on behalf of His people, even of His anxiety in the garden, is that *His people may have peace, so that prayer might be the solution to their worries.* All the unbelieving worries for today and for tomorrow, all the sin that lies in mistrust of God, He replaces with, "Peace I leave with you, my peace I give unto you: not as the world giveth, give I unto you. Let not your heart be troubled, neither let it be afraid" (John 14:27).

Sometimes we read the words in this text as if they were one of those little sayings on a calendar page, a billboard, or a greeting card—a glib and superficial bit of advice that you can take or leave. That's not how it should be read. These two verses are like the gentle words of an embracing heavenly Father, whispered to His anxiety-ridden child who has died a thousand deaths, all in vain, having worried so needlessly, endlessly, and foolishly, until he or she runs to Calvary and dives into His arms to hear Him say: "My child, why did you fear? Where is your faith? If I spared not my only begotten Son, will I not freely give you all that you need?"

Turn from Your Sins and Rest in Jesus Christ

People who are not reconciled with God but are still at enmity with Him have every reason to be careful. You should worry, but not about the things you are worrying about so often—food, drink, money, your future, your job, your health, your place in the world. You need to worry about your soul, your sin, your danger, and your place in eternity. When you do not seek the kingdom of God first with its righteousness, then the only thing that is added to you is sorrow and a just anxiety for your future.

Without the secure footing Calvary provides to sinners, you have no security: "There is no peace, saith my God, to the wicked" (Isa. 57:21). But know this: it is not by worrying that you will ever be saved. You need to run from your sins and rest in Christ alone. Apart from Him there is no safety, even if you could worry your way through a million worlds. Such worry only adds to your guilt. Every day you are outside of Christ, you add daily to your debt.

But the gospel still comes to you and says this: there is pardon, peace, a reconciled God, faith, confidence, and access all through Jesus Christ, His shed blood and righteousness. There is peace that can garrison you all the days of your earthly pilgrimage and through death, to the presence of God forever. How you need Calvary, Christ, and all that He has obtained for daily living as well—not a life of care, but a life of prayer.

The blessing promised in this text is really a double one. The burden of worry is replaced by the double blessing of *prayer* and *peace*. Think about how God is knocking on the door of your life right now to get your attention. What is the difficulty, the problem, the grief, the impossibility that confronts you just now? What are you struggling with? What occupies your mind? Instead of tempting you to worry (for God tempts no man to sin), God is saying, "I'm calling you to pray—to talk to me, to tell me your burdens and roll them on me and leave them with me." All we have to do is come, to both let God hear our voice and to listen to Him through His word. What a God the Christian has! Nothing is too great for Him; nothing is too small for Him. We can present any trouble of our hearts, any burden of our lives to Him.

COMPREHENSIVE PEACE

As we take a look back to this glorious peace the Bible promises, notice how comprehensive it is. Be careful for *nothing,* but in *everything*...." Notice the contrast. We aren't called to be careful to let our request be made known to God for a few things or even in most things. Paul says *nothing* and *everything*. There is never a time for worry. There is always a time for prayer. There is never any place for worry. There is always a place for prayer.

When we live with this focus, obedient to God's command, we may expect this peace that passes understanding. It may come in fits and starts; it may be interrupted in our lives; sometimes it may not seem to be within our reach in our experience. But the Scriptures say God will give a peace that surpasses our understanding. Our hope is not in our experience, but in God and His promises.

What does God mean by a peace that passes all understanding? It means that it is impossible to wrap your mental arms around this peace. When we experience it, we can't really figure out where it comes from, why it is so strong, why it gives so much confidence. It's like the apostle says: It "passeth all understanding." So often in our worries, we bind ourselves to our own understanding of events, which is so miniscule, so limited. We cannot see past ourselves. We look for peace in human places, but we don't go higher up. But God can give us a peace, not one that falls short of our understanding or accords with our understanding, but *passes* all understanding. Won't this call for believers' praise to all eternity?

CONCLUSION

It is my prayer that this explanation of Paul's teaching on care will help you to experience God's peace as you believingly look away from yourself to God, His character, and His promises. Don't forget that God's word is always faithful. It has proved its faithfulness throughout millennia. Many self-help approaches come and go, but God's word abides forever. God's word unmasks our sin and unbelief, and it is hard to have them exposed. Yet through this process, God settles His people more and more on Himself. Trials serve to that end in the lives of God's children.

Sometimes we grow despondent because we have unrealistic expectations of ourselves. Just like small children should not be frustrated if they can't ride a bike with as much ease as they see others doing it, or those who have just taken up running can't run marathons like those who have done so for years—so too believers should refrain from comparing themselves to others.

Each of us is unique in our make-up, task, and calling in this world. God has gifted everyone differently in the body of Christ; we should seek to help and equip others around us, realizing that with Christ we are never alone. Sometimes a long fight with anxiety can make us empathize and help others who are going through the profoundly unsettling experience of constant worry. Even if it is the case, by God's grace, that anxiety seems a distant memory, don't grow impatient with those who suffer greatly with anxiety. Think of where you were once, or where you might be if your circumstances or background or personality make-up were different. Be sure to listen carefully and prayerfully to people as they trust you with their anxieties and worries. Don't mock or make them feel ashamed of their worries. They are trusting you with sensitive things; you can make them feel more alone if they find that you won't sit with them and listen. I have learned that people fighting a minute-by-minute battle with anxiety are usually far stronger than I am. I have learned a lot from them about the grace of God and the endurance that God has given to them in their struggle.

Never forget that God is worthy to be trusted and served. As we pursue God's ways, looking to God's grace, He has promised to fulfill all His counsel in our lives, to His praise and glory.